How To Be

Lie Detector

"The <u>Truth</u> Is You're Being Lied To!"

How To Become a Human...

LIE

DETECTOR

Simon Hodgkinson

YES   NO

Get The TRUTH Out Of Anyone...
In Any Situation...
Even If They Never Say A Single Word

Lie Detector

About 'Lie Dectector'
Published In the United Kingdom by
Hodgkinson Publishing Limited
© Copyright Hodgkinson Publishing Ltd
2010 All Rights Reserved

Online: HodgkinsonPublishing.com

Table Of Contents

Let's Lie Together, Shall We?

"He who permits himself to tell a lie once, finds it much easier to do it a second and third time, till at length it becomes habitual."

Thomas Jefferson

Everybody lies. *Especially* those who claim that they never lie.

Sure, there may be a *handful* of people on this entire planet who *never* lie. And, heck, maybe there are a few smaller, lesser-known cultures, in some remote areas of this planet, where lying is unheard of, or at least a rare occurrence.

However, in this society, it seems that lies are a 'normal' part of our communication, and way of life.

We lie to our parents, they lie to us. We lie to our children, they lie to us. We lie to our friends, neighbors, relatives, significant others, bosses, peers, competitors... everybody lies.

So, much so that we have even created *categories* of different types of lying: white lies, noble lies, contextual lies, fabrication, exaggeration, lying by omission, perjury...etc. etc.

A lot of time, money, and resources are wasted everyday, by almost everyone, simply because they are not being honest with each other.

Just think back of your past dealings with others. How many dates, relationships and business dealings do you wish you could have handled different if you had all the facts from Day 1?

How many of those relationships and

partnerships would you have ended much sooner than you actually did?

How much of your time, and life, was wasted because certain relationships or business acquaintances weren't honest and forthright with you from the very beginning?

It all adds up over time, to quite a huge chunk of your life.

And, while we would love to always be told the truth, so that our resulting choices and decisions don't end up costing us time, money, and wasted resources, the harsh reality is that we live in a world of deception.

Yet, when it really matters, all communication - whether business or personal - has to be built on honesty. Without it, no real progress can be made.

So, whether we want to or not, being able to get to the truth is often a <u>necessity</u>.

The better you are at it, the more it will benefit you, your business, and your life.

The Biggest Lie of All

"If you do not tell the truth about
yourself you cannot tell it about other
people"
Virginia Woolf

I've spent more than half my life studying
human motivation, persuasion, seduction,
marketing, hypnosis, NLP, etc.

And, one of my most powerful insights I had
during these years that benefited me (and
others) the most had nothing to do with
what (or who) we were dealing with
externally. Instead, the most important piece
was in understanding what was going on
inside of us, within the inner recesses of *our
own mind*.

Filtering, Editing and Deleting

Whether we would like to admit to it or not,
none of us see reality as it really is.

In fact, there is so much going on around us simultaneously, at all times, it's *impossible* for our brain to process everything.

Therefore, we have been trained to process a *limited* amount of information at any given time.

For example, if we're in a crowded room where everyone is talking at the same time, and several pools of conversation are occurring simultaneously, we can't possibly follow every conversation even if we can hear all of them. It would be like trying to watch five TV screens at once, all with different shows on.

So, we decide which ones to filter out and which one(s) to pay attention to. While the rest of the conversations are still going on, we simply delete, edit or filter them out.

But, here's what's interesting...

Different people edit, delete and filter out different information based on their own *preset* internal filters, beliefs, preferences, and biases.

Consequently, we often tend to miss certain important pieces of information, either be default or on purpose (if the information doesn't serve our best interest.)

In other words, sometimes we never get to the truth because we don't want to hear it. We'd rather believe the lie.

Think of that nice young lady whose lover always cheats on her. Everybody knows it and tries to tell her that the guy is a liar and a cheater. Yet, she refuses to believe it.

It's not that she can't see the signs herself. She can. It's not that she didn't know from the moment he first started cheating on her. On some level, she did. But, her mind simply edited those parts out. Because she's happier believing the lie than accepting the bitter truth.

The biggest lies are the lies that we tell ourselves.

It doesn't make any sense, does it? Why would she lie to herself like that?

Yet, the reality is, we all do this to ourselves - *on some level.* (Whether we'd like to believe it or not.)

We keep buying exercise contraptions, weight loss programs and pills because we keep wanting to believe that it will work - or that 'this time' we'll actually use it.

We continue to spend money on 'get rich quick' schemes and tell ourselves that finally we'll find one that actually works and starts pouring cash into our bank accounts with the push of a button.

We make donations to certain organizations and believe that most of the money will actually go to the needy.

And those are just the common lies.

Most of us don't know, nor do we care, about all the lies that we tell ourselves. In fact, some of the lies actually help us lead a happier and saner life.

But when it comes to getting the truth out of others, we have to at least be *aware* of the filters and mechanisms that are already set up in *our* head.

No matter what we do in life, everything starts first in our own minds. So, until we know what's going on *inside* us, there's no way of ever knowing what's really going on *outside* of us and around us.

Unless we know what's going on in our own heads, there's no way we will ever know what's going on in another person's head.

Everything that we see, hear, taste, smell, and feel is filtered through our existing beliefs, assumptions, and biases.

In other words, the biggest lies are the ones that we tell **ourselves**!

None of us want to hear this. Yet, unless you take care of this all important first step, nothing else will work.

Imagine trying to look inside someone's car...

How well would you be able to see inside the car if you were wearing a dirty or fogged up pair of sun glasses?

Not very well, wouldn't you agree?

It wouldn't matter how clear the window of the car was. You still wouldn't be able to see inside it, unless you first cleaned your glasses.

Here are some things to be aware of that will help keep the fog off our own glasses...

The Blind Man Sees Most Clearly

"The greatest deception men suffer is from their own opinions."
Leonardo Da Vinci

If you want to get to the truth, go into the situation blind!

That means, you have to put your assumptions, biases, preconceived notions, ego, and especially your emotions, aside.

A person who is prejudice against a particular ethnicity will walk in believing that the individual of that particular ethnicity is the most likely suspect.

And as such, he will probably let the real culprit slip away while he's busy focusing on who he thinks *should* be the most likely suspect. (The worst part is, oftentimes, this person will not be aware of how many his personal beliefs and biases are clouding his decisions.)

A person who has always had bad luck with women and has had his past 3 girl friends cheat on him will go in believing that the female suspect is the mostly likely to lie and cheat.

A person who has been treated unfairly by the police would very likely assume that if the case involves a police officer, then the officer is the guilty party...case closed.

Assume nothing, accuse no one, and do not let anyone use your emotions to nudge you towards a particular direction.

Most people are quick to fall for the emotional traps when the opposite sex is involved.

A beautiful woman, especially one who makes it look like she's interested in the man, will make a man believe, and do, almost anything she wants.

Similarly, an attractive man could use the same lame pickup line on a woman that a not-so-attractive man just used on her, unsuccessfully, 2 minutes ago. Yet, in the attractive man's case, that same line will work on the woman.

The emotion that's affecting people's judgment and decisions in the above two cases is clearly "lust."

Other emotions can be used in similar ways.

A person who compliments or praises someone (about looks, attire, style, or whatever) may be able to get away with a lot more than another person who didn't pay any compliments.

A person acting like someone's biggest fan may be able to get his autograph, time, or more... where others may not be able to get anywhere.

Negative emotions can also be used to sway people into making decisions or judgments...fear being one of the biggest ones of them all.

To summarize, be aware of any emotions you're feeling during your search for the truth.

And... be aware of any individual that tries to appeal to one of your emotions...be it ego, love, fear or anything else.

If you feel you can't put your anger, attraction, or other emotions aside temporarily, let someone else handle that particular truth-seeking mission.

Once you have taken note of what's going on inside you, and taken the steps to not let that influence your process, it's time to focus on what's going on externally.

Let's go over some of the tips, tools and techniques you can use for that...

Getting To Know You

"You can fool some of the people all of the time, and all of the people some of the time, but you cannot fool all of the people all of the time."
Abraham Lincoln

I used to hang out with an amazing poker player. Let's call him "Jim," for the purpose of this section.

His strategy was to study his opponents for at least 30 minutes (and up to an hour, if possible) before starting to bet large sums of money on the table.

During those first 30 - 60 minutes, which he called the "gathering intelligence" phase, he would covertly but carefully study the cues, ticks, gestures, and every other body movement and facial expressions of the other players that he could gather.

(For those in the know, 30 - 60 minutes isn't really a lot of time to study another person, especially if you're studying 3 different players at the same time. But, as I said, this guy was very good.)

See, he wanted to study these guys in their 'comfort' phase, in their natural habitat if you will, when their actions and gestures weren't influenced by uneasiness, fear, or any other additional emotions.

Then...when they did have something to worry about or fear i.e. when he started betting big money against them, many of the gestures and cues they'd exhibit would be clear as day for Jim to pick up on.

Many expert interrogators use a similar strategy.

They start off by being very friendly and accommodating to the suspect. They talk about normal stuff. While they're doing this, they get to build some level of rapport with the suspect AND they get a chance to study the suspect in his/her "natural" or normal condition....as natural as it could be, in that situation anyway.

Many would go a step further and work on building comfort, and even assure the suspect that there's really nothing to worry about and they are in no trouble at all. They would then spend several minutes studying the person while they were in a comfortable state.

They would pay attention to how the person talked, their body language, their heart rate, etc.

Once they had all this information, they would use it as the model to compare to the changes that would occur *after* they would start the interrogation.

We'll go over what changes they would look for, in further detail, below.

As we do that, keep in mind that many of these changes, signs, or "tells" may not necessarily mean much *individually*. Just one of those signs being present may not be enough to assume that the person is lying.

To get accurate results, you will often need more than just one sign. The more of them that you get, the more accurate your results and conclusions will be.

One final piece of advice before we start breaking down all the individual signs and techniques you can use to catch a liar...

<u>Important</u>: When you do start noticing some initial signs of someone telling you a lie, do **not** let him/her know that you are on to them. If you let them know that you've caught them in a lie, they will become very careful and guarded from that point on. And, they will do they best to not get caught in any other lies or reveal any further information to you.

If your goal is to gather as much information and facts from him as you possibly can, let him believe that everything is fine. Do not let him find out that you're there to catch him on his lies. The longer you let this go on, the longer he will keep his guard down, and the longer you will be able to get more info and evidence from him.

Only after you've gathered some solid evidence should you decide whether or not to confront him right there.

Sometimes, you may have to take the info you pulled from him and use it on another suspect, without letting either of them know what you're up to.

In those instances, you may not want to confront the first person about his lies even after you're done questioning him. Chances are that you may have to go back to him at a later time to ask him more questions.

So, do not let anyone know what you're up to until you're absolutely sure that you've got all the information and evidence that you need.

Now...let's talk about all the signs, clues and 'tells' that you can use to catch liars in the act...

Note: We'll start with the more commonly-known stuff and then move on to the other not-so-commonly-known things...

Read My Lips: No New Lies

"Man is least himself when he talks in his own person. Give him a mask, and he will tell you the truth."
Oscar Wilde

Many of us believe that the actual *words* a liar chooses to use is not all that important since "they will all be lies anyway."

In reality, *what* a person says - and *how* he says it - can often reveal a lot...even when he's telling lies.

Also, often times, what a person *isn't* saying can speak volumes.

Keep in mind that you may not always have a person in front of you, face to face, when you're talking to him. Some conversations may have to be done over the phone, through a cubicle partition, etc.

In the above cases especially, it becomes vitally important to pay close attention to what the person is saying, and how he's saying it. Because his words may be all that you have to go by.

On the surface, a liar may be saying one thing, but his *choice* of words and the *delivery* of those words may often reveal something entirely different.

A very simple example of this can be when a person is asked a question and he responds with, "Uh huh..." instead of a confident, resounding "YES." Or the person may simply *nod* his head in the 'yes' motion instead of saying any words out loud. (Think of how a child usually responds when he/she is in trouble, and compare that to how he would respond when he's confident, happy, and has nothing to hide. There's a big difference between the two responses.)

Let's discuss this further...

Slip & Slide

Of course, one of the more commonly-known giveaways of a lie or cover-up is the 'Freudian Slip.' It is when a word 'slips out' during conversation that reveals the speaker's real thoughts or intentions.

Example: A guy is married to a woman who is a vegetarian, and is obligated to (or maybe even pressured into) not eating any meat. One evening he comes home late (after secretly wolfing down a hamburger) and the wife asks, "Are you hungry, or did you eat?"

The guy replies, "Yes, I did meat...uh...**eat**... I did *eat*...already....thanks!"

Since the word 'meat'...or the intent to *not* reveal that word...was his primary thought, it easily slipped out during conversation, without him having much control over it.

Zero to 60 in Two Sentences

One of the most common ways a liar tries to cover his lies is by blurting out a response to your questions as quickly as he possibly can.

People generally believe that if they take too long to answer the question, it will appear as if they're lying. So, to counteract that, they often tend to answer a little *too* quickly...much faster than what's considered normal. And, in doing so, they reveal that something's just not right.

Still Talking

Since liars often talk too fast, they also tend to talk too much. You may have already experienced this in real life or in movies (usually comedy shows.)

Example: Instead of just saying,

"No, I didn't do it,"

A liar will often rush to say something like,

"No, I didn't do it...How could you ask me that...I would never do that...I can't believe you'd think I would do that...I wasn't even in town that day..."

This could go on for a while...

(There's a reason why attorneys often advise their clients to "be brief." They know that the more a person talks, the more chances there are of him revealing something.)

Basically, the liar is trying too hard to convince you that he's not guilty. As a result, he's over-doing his responses. Oftentimes, he is also trying to convince you *quickly*, so that you can move on to another subject as quickly as possible.

For the same reasons, a liar's answers could also be short...too short. For example, when asked if he did it, he may simply respond with, "No" or just shake his head from side-to-side to signify a 'no.'

This really isn't confusing provided you keep the main intent of the liar in mind: he is trying to rush things, to get it over with as quickly as possible, and either move on to something else or escape the scene. (We will build on all of this in later sections.)

Whenever someone is trying to finish the conversation in a hurry, or change the subject to something else, there's a good chance that they're hiding something.

There are, however, a few exceptions to this rule...

If a person *extends* his sentence by emphasizing words like "not," there's a good chance that he is trying to emphasize the point that he did "not" do it, or was "not" involved in anyway. In these cases, there's a good chance that more digging should be done.

Example: Instead of saying, "I didn't do it," he will say, "I did **not** do it."

Emphasizing the "not" can often be a sign that he's trying too hard to convince you.

The Loudest Bark

It is said that the smaller the dog, the louder its bark is. And, the reason for this is so that the smaller dog can 'appear' ferocious, when in fact it really may not be much of a danger at all. By barking louder, it is compensating for its small size.

Similarly, when a person is trying too hard or

too much to convince you of something, oftentimes the opposite is true.

I've known someone who would always make it a point to say,

"I just can't lie. I don't know how. I'm not very good at it."

These types of phrases were being repeated a little too often, and would sometimes be snuck into conversations where it didn't quite fit.

And, the repetition of those phrases was exactly what made me suspicious and eventually gave this person away. The repetition got my attention and caused me to start looking for more signs and evidence that I probably wouldn't have thought to look for otherwise.

This same person turned out to be the biggest liar I had ever met.

If they're trying too hard, there's a reason for it and you should start paying attention to other subtle clues.

You may also hear phrases like,

"I don't know anything. Stop asking me all these questions."

There's a good chance that this person is afraid he will give something away the longer he is made to answer more questions (which is often the end result of interrogations.)

He may very likely be someone who can be broken easily and therefore wants to convince you that he doesn't know anything, hoping that you would stop asking.

In contrast, a confident and/or innocent person will be happy to answers as many questions as needed to clear their selves, and maybe even help the situation with what he can.

He may even go as far as to empathize with you, if the situation surrounding the investigation is a negative one.

(More on this later.)

That's Just Wrong

Similar to the above technique of "trying to hard" to convince you of his answer, a liar may also add something about his beliefs or stance into his answers to convince you that it just isn't in his nature to commit what he's being accused of.

Example: If the issue is discrimination, and the person is asked whether he made a racist remark toward someone, he may respond with,

"Absolutely not! I feel that racists are the worst kind of scum on the planet."....or...."No way. I'm a Christian, and a true Christian would never judge others."

He feels that just saying "no" won't be enough to persuade you of his innocence, so, once again, he is trying harder than normal to convince you...not only by denying the accusation but by 'going the extra mile' and adding moral or religious statements about himself (none of which are true about his beliefs, of course.)

Could it simply be that the person makes the

above 'additional' statements because he really feels strongly about those things? Sure, it's possible. And that's why we discussed earlier the importance of collecting more than just one clue or sign.

If just one of the above clues is present, that may not necessarily mean that the person is lying or guilty. It's always best to establish patterns and collect as many of clues and slip ups as possible. The more you have, the more sure you can be of your conclusions.

Well, That Depends...

Former President Bill Clinton made headlines when he responded to a question by saying,

"It depends on what the definition of "is" is."

When the person you're questioning starts giving answers similar to the one above, it does not automatically mean that he's lying or hiding something. *However*, as a general rule, it is also a good idea to do some additional digging because it's very likely that they're trying to hide something or get away with technicalities.

Here are a few other examples of responses similar to the one above...

"I couldn't tell you." (Does that mean he doesn't know? Or that he's not supposed to tell you?)

"I can't say." (Same as above)

"I am not aware of any official findings." (What about "unofficial" findings? What about findings that haven't been made public yet?)

"It depends on how you look at it." (This response can be given in almost any situation, and is almost always a clue to dig further.)

"It depends on ___(fill in the blanks)____" (See above.)

"Can I ask why you're asking about that?" (This can be a way to deflect attention, stall for time, etc. - we will discuss those individually, in later sections.)

"Can I ask what your interest in that is?"
(Same as above.)

"Can you be more specific?" (Same as above. Could also be a genuine clarity request.)

"I'm not sure I understand the question."
(Same as above.)

"What exactly are you asking me?" (Same as above.)

"Where did you hear that?" (Trying to find out if the source is worth worrying about. And stalling.)

"That's a good question." (Stalling for time.)

"I think we both know the answer to that." (Trying to get you to choose an answer that's in his favour. Appealing to - and also somewhat challenging – your ego and intellect.)

"I think the answer to that is obvious." (Same as above.)

The Silent Treatment

Unless we're among friends or loved ones, most of us aren't comfortable with long periods of silence.

And since a liar being interrogated is often pretty uncomfortable to begin with, silence only makes matters worse for him.

A great strategy that interrogators, and even many sales people, use is to ask a question (or make a statement), then wait for the person to answer. After the person has answered, you would maintain your silence.

Of course, the liar, becoming uneasy with the uncomfortable silence will decide to talk some more, thinking that his initial answer wasn't satisfactory and convincing.

He will often continue talking and adding to his original statement until you finally say something.

Example:

You: Do you know anything about last night's robbery?
Him: No, I do not.
You: [....remain silent...]
Him: I was home all night.
You: [....remain silent...]
Him: I wasn't even up late.
You: [....remain silent...]
Him: I just watched some TV and went to bed.

This could go on until you respond, which would make him feel like you're finally satisfied with his story. And, it's a sign that the person is guilty or is trying to hide something.

Often, you will end up getting info (like his additional statements above) that you can use to poke holes into his story later.

Obviously, a person who has nothing to hide won't share information in spurts. He will just come out and lay it all out.

Beware of a statement that sounds too rehearsed or polished, without any of the natural pauses or joiners that tend to occur during normal conversation. If it sounds rehearsed, it probably is.

Say It, But Not Like That

We've already established that the words being spoken can offer many clues as to the speaker's true intentions and emotions.

Moreover, the *delivery* of those words...how they are spoken... the volume, pitch, speed of the speaker...delays or pauses...which word is stressed or emphasized more...all of these can offer additional clues as to the speaker's intended meaning. Subtle changes in any of the above can alter the meaning of the words substantially.

If a person hesitates, or delays answering a question, it can often mean that he's processing and running the possible answers through his head in order to pick the right one.

The same can be true if a person answers the first part quickly (with a yes or no response) but pauses to deliver the rest of it (the explanation to the first part of the answer.)

Example:

You: You happened to miss class yesterday, didn't you?
Him: Yes........I couldn't make it....I wasn't feeling well.

You: How do you feel about having a female as your superior?
Him: .....[pause]...Fine....no problem at all....I've had female supervisors before.

You: What did you have for breakfast today?
Him: .....[pause]...Oh the usual....nothing fancy.... coffee...and toast.

(Notice the deliberate "filler" answers preceding the actual answer... most likely used so the speaker has enough time to think of a sellable answer, reason or explanation.)

Fibbing Fundamentalist

It's no secret that fundamentalists often tend to believe the exact opposite of what they're passionate and furious about.

People who are most disgusted by the gay and lesbian lifestyle are often discovered to be closeted homosexuals themselves. (Also, many times, they haven't fully accepted this part of themselves on a conscious level. And, they are often disgusted even by the thought of such a possibility. So, they feel an inner need to aggressively protest against it, outwardly, in an attempt to keep the truth hidden and buried deep inside themselves.)

Individuals preaching the loudest about religion, punishing non-believers, etc. are often struggling with the worst inner demons themselves.

By exaggerating his own display of passion, hatred, or whatever is fitting, such a person is trying to cover up the exact thing in himself that he is protesting about. And, he's also hoping to convince others of his false motive, belief, etc.

Note: The above examples are not *always* true. But they are true often enough to warrant a closer look such individuals whenever they are somehow related to the investigation (or situation) at hand.

And, of course, as mentioned earlier, other clues and pieces have to fit into the big picture in order to build a solid case or make firm assumptions.

Personally Detached

If a person is being dishonest, he will tend to detach himself from the situation or certain parts of that situation.

Example: Instead of saying,

"Yes, I prepared dinner at home that night," he may say, "Yes, dinner was prepared at home that night."

Notice how he subtly detaches himself personally by not using the word "I."

Note: There was nothing about his preparing dinner that could have gotten him into trouble. However, since his objective his to hide certain facts or lie about certain things, his brain automatically distances him even from simple statements that really have nothing to do with anything.

Similarly, he may also say,

"Yes, I was in my bedroom all night," he may say, "Yes...was in the bedroom all night."

Again notice the subtle detachment by not using the words "I" or "my."

Remember, not wanting to use these words is not a conscious decision on his part. He may not even realize that he's doing this. Yet, if you know to pay attention to these subtle shifts, you can learn a lot about the person and get to the real story.

Also, there won't be too many (or any) tonal and volume shifts in the person's speech, if he's lying.

As mentioned earlier, when we're having a normal conversation, we tend to stress certain words more than others or even drag certain words out longer than needed. We don't plan for this, it just happens to match how we're feeling and what we're thinking at the time.

But, when a person is lying, his entire sentence (or speech) would be monotonic, without much emphasis on certain words or changes in volume.

The above is similar to instances where you may say to someone, "Wow, that was a great movie, wasn't it?" And the other person may reply with, "Yeah....uh huh....great" without any tonal or volume shifts in the response, i.e. void of any positive emotion.

Can You Repeat That?

In an earlier section, we mentioned that a liar may sometimes cover his mouth with a hand in order to hold back or mask his own words, without realizing that he's doing so.

If he doesn't use his hand for this, he can also accomplish the same effect simply by mumbling or speaking too softly for anyone to really understand what he's saying.

Oftentimes, the interrogator may have to

say, "Please repeat that" or "Speak louder please."

In contrast, when you're passionate and sure about what you want to say, your voice may actually be slightly louder, and reveal the excitement.

Are You Asking Or Telling

Another sign of a person being unsure or dishonest about what he's saying is when his answer comes out sounding like a question.

Example: You may ask him, "Where were you on the night of the accident?" and he may respond by saying, "At home....?" in the form of a question instead of a confident statement.

See, in his head, he was probably *asking* himself, "Should I say I was at home or at the office?"...and while his brain was in the "questioning" frame, his answer comes out in the form of a question.

Also, it may come out sounding like a

question because he's not entirely sure if you would buy his answer completely. So, without realizing, he's somewhat *asking* you if that answer will be satisfactory.

Oftentimes, he may try to quickly correct the mistake by repeating, "At home...I was at home."

Body of Lies

"80% of what you understand in a conversation is read through the body, not the words."
Deborah Bull

Parents are great at spotting lies from children, especially if it's their own children. They may not know exactly what to look for on a conscious level. But, on a sub-conscious level, their mind knows and picks up on subtle clues that the conscious mind may not see.

The reason is simple.

Our body doesn't lie. It can't lie. (There is a very small group of individuals who have trained and conditioned their bodies to hide the lie signals. But, the rest of world is not able to control their body on such a deep level. Many of them don't even know what their own lying signals are, let alone try to hide them. In fact, many people don't even know - nor believe - that the body is revealing everything that they're trying so hard to hide.)

It's also important to recognize that we already use our body to communicate, even when we're not lying. We use our eyes, our facial expressions, and our arms to get our point across.

So, it's only logical to pay attention to these communication aids when we're trying to get to the truth.

As mentioned earlier, while everyone is great at telling lies by using the words they choose, most people haven't figured out how to stop their bodies from revealing those lies.

Eye Spy With My Little "I"

You may have heard that the eyes are windows to our soul. This is certainly true when you're trying to get to the soul of a person's true intent and feelings.

Without realizing it at the time, people feel

that others will be able to see their true feelings by looking into their eyes. Or they may simply feel guilty, embarrassed, or scared of facing you.

For any of those reasons, a person who is lying will do his best to avoid making eye contact with you. He will look everywhere except directly at you. Looking down or quickly moving his eyes side-to-side are common signs.

Let Me Hear Your Body Talk

Since we already use our arms and hands as additional communication aids, to gesture and punctuate with, we try not to use them as much when we're lying - in an effort to not reveal the truth.

And, it is by doing exactly that that we tend to reveal what we think we're hiding.

Clenched fists, hidden in pockets, folded arms can all be signs of restraint or defensiveness, implying that lying may be involved...or at least that the speaker is nervous or unsure about the validity of his statements.

If any of the above happens when a person is asked a question, the same can be assumed of the person's intent.

The more sure and passionate we are of what you're saying, the more our arms and hands tend to move and gesture.

Arms and legs tucked close to the body and/or crossed/folded can also be signs that the person is trying to keep things 'close' to himself, that he is keeping something from being revealed.

The above can also be a sign of discomfort, uneasiness or insecurity. (When we're comfortable and relaxed, our body is also more comfortable, relaxed, loose, and moving freely...instead of being tucked in tight.)

Also, if we're asked a question that we don't know anything about (read: we don't have any reason to lie about,) our reaction will be that of confusion or curiosity, i.e. unclenched fists, unfolded arms, palms upward, etc.

Facial expressions would often match the reaction, also.

In general, body movements that seem restrained, held back, or even forced are all signs that something is not right. (A *partial* smile or attempt at laughter, hands and arms attempting to move yet seeming to be held back, and movements that seem mechanical or stiff/unnatural are some examples.)

Forced or partial movements can also mean that the person is *trying* to appear normal and natural, but is actually giving himself away by doing so.

Whether we realize it consciously or not, our body is always communicating our true feelings, even when our words are trying very hard to hide those feelings.

Touchy, Touchy

While talking, if the person happens to touch his face, nose, ear, throat, or back of neck, it can mean that he is not being entirely honest. Covering the mouth, while speaking, is also a sign that he is not sure of or doesn't believe in what he is saying....or that he is trying to hide or hold information in. (Remember, these movements are all done on an unconscious level and reveals what the mind is really thinking, so the person is unaware of the movements.)

Ticks and Tells

You've probably heard of or seen people who have certain ticks or tells that indicate that they're telling a lie. These are involuntary responses that the person cannot control even when he is made aware of it.

For example, a person's right eye can start twitching when he lies. And while this tick is rare and very specific to the individual, there are more general signs that apply to a larger percentage of the population.

Here are a few of these...

Skin tone can change when a person is caught in a lie, or an embarrassing situation; His face can become flushed and appear red. As hard as he may try, there's no easy way to control or hide this.

Breathing rate can increase quickly and become very shallow. The person may even try to counteract this by taking slower and deeper breaths...and give himself away.

Perspiration is also a commonly known response; a person under pressure can often start to perspire significantly, even if the temperature of the room is *below* a comfortable setting. This, again, is a response that he will have no control over.

Trembling uncontrollably is also a common sign and can be noticed especially in the person's hands during nervousness or fear. And, again, this can happen even if the room temperature is comfortable or even warmer than normal.

Throat clearing, coughing, or even swallowing. This apparently happens because mucus forms in the throat in the presence of anxiety, and also, the person's vocal chords tend to tighten when he is experiencing stress.

So I Dub Thee Unbelievable

Have you ever watched those old martial arts movies where the voices were dubbed (in English) over the original voice track (in Chinese or Japanese?) Didn't the timing of the dubbed voices seem off when compared to the body and facial movements of the speaker?

Timing is hard to fake, unless you're a very good actor, or have had lots of practice deceiving others (which, in the end is about being a good actor and/or being able to embody the character you've adopted, for the moment.)

Imagine watching a person making a passionate speech and pounding on the table to punctuate certain points of his speech. That would appear pretty passionate to us, right?

Now, imagine the person doing the same

passionate speech but pounding on the table a second or two *after* he delivers the line. Would you agree that something would seem 'off' when the pounding was delayed, or didn't appear to be in sync with the person's vocal shift?

Yes. And that's because when a person is trying to *appear* emotional, the pounding (or other vigorous hand/arm movements) are forced and not a spontaneous occurrence. The arm movement(s) is being forced or faked, which means something is up.

This is true of all movements, gestures and facial expressions. Example: if a person speaks a sentence (or paragraph) and then does a smile or grin a moment or two later, again, the timing is off - which means he is consciously and deliberately delivering the smile/grin...and something is not right.

When we're talking naturally and freely, a smile, laugh, or even arm/hand movements just happen spontaneously. It doesn't have to be planned. And it happens in perfect timing to the rest of our actions and words.

We don't usually talk and then smile a

second later. We either smile as we're talking....or we may even smile a moment or two *before* we start speaking, and maintain the smile during.

The same is true for any other emotion. If we're angry, our words will match our gestures. We don't deliver the sentence and *then* display an angry facial expression 3 seconds *later*.

When the timing is off, it's as if the person delivers his speech and then decides *later* that he'd better add the movements and expressions to match what he just said. And, in doing so, he reveals that something is not right, that he's masking or hiding something.

While we're discussing the subject of 'timing'...

Also, pay close attention to the *initial* timing...the person's absolute *first* reaction...if you'd like to get to his/her real feelings.

Example: If someone has been given bad news, he generally shows a sign of grief, sadness and sorrow. But, if there's a slightest hint of a smile or joy immediately before he expresses the negative emotion, there's a very good chance that his negative expressions are manufactured.

He was smart enough to *attempt* to display his outer reaction to convey his (fake) emotions, but there was still a glimpse of the unconscious reaction that would give him away.

(Oftentimes, we pick up on these little clues but don't realize that we did. The result is, we get that 'feeling' inside that "something just isn't right"...that you're not sure you can believe what the other person said you.)

Similarly, if a person starts to smile (or frown, or whatever) a moment before he starts speaking, it's safe to assume that it's a genuine reaction matching his true emotions.

In other words, we are emotional creatures. Our words always follow our emotions, not the other way around. We feel the emotion first and then try to express it through words. We don't say "I feel so happy" first, and feel the emotion afterwards.

Sometimes, there's even a delay before any words are spoken. You'll see the emotion being expressed by the person's face and body...and the words will follow only after he is able to find a way to express himself verbally.

Certain emotions can also render us speechless, at least for a few moments before we're able to recover.

If the emotion (and the outer, physical reaction) *matches* the words that follow, even if the words are slightly delayed, it's all good.

And, of course, the actual gesture has to match the emotion and/or speech. If someone is telling you that everything is okay while frowning or showing other facial signs of negative emotions, clearly something is not right.

Also, the gesture has to be *complete*, if it is real. A half a smile, a lame attempt at a shoulder shrug, etc. are all considered incomplete gestures, and are often a result of the person forcing those gestures.

Similarly, if a smile is genuine, the person's entire face moves and changes. Teeth are also fully exposed. If it's a fake smile, only the mouth area will move/change. Lips may be very slightly parted or not parted at all. No change would be seen in other areas of the face.

The same is true for other emotions. (When we genuinely express anger, again, it can be seen in our entire face. The skin may appear flushed and red. In some people, veins pop out. These things can't be easily faked.)

Just Exactly How Surprised Are You

It's also helpful to keep in mind that various emotions can last for different durations.

Laughter, for example, can last for a few moments, or a few minutes. It can even start again after stopping for a few moments.

In contrast, surprise comes and goes very quickly. That means, if someone continues to look and act surprised much longer than normal (after you've delivered the surprising news,) it may be done just to throw you off. (This isn't true 100% of the time, but is usually accurate.)

Assume The Lying Position

Overall body positioning can also reveal a lot about a person.

Typically, when we are relaxed and/or confident, and have nothing to worry about, our body reflects that mental frame. Our posture will be erect, confident, or at least relaxed. The alpha position, portraying confidence, will also take up more space by spreading out.

If a person is insecure, unsure of himself, or has something to worry about or hide, his posture will also reflect that. He will tend to be hunched over, avoiding eye contact, arms tucked in close to the body or hands in pocket, etc. (The opposite of the alpha position.)

Of course, if the person is generally insecure, and not very confident to begin with, his posture will already be somewhat weak, even before he is approached with questions, accusations, etc.

In those instances, watch for other cues outlined above, as well as for the overall posture to become even weaker, i.e. limbs tucking in even closer to the body, etc.

It's also common for the person to not exhibit hands with open palms and extended fingers. There won't be any pointing going on at all. No big (outward) arm movements.

Two Steps Backward...

Similarly, when a person is relaxed, confident, and/or passionate about himself or his message, he will stand facing you, look you straight in the eyes, and will even move closer to you (without realizing) in order to impress his ideas and views upon you. (Just think of how good friends or peers communicate. They don't sit as far away from each other as possible.)

However....when a person has something to

hide or is lying to you, he will tend to *increase* the distance between you and him, broadcasting his intention of wanting to distance himself from you. This may often happen very subtly, either by use of a quick short step back, body swayed back a bit, or even the head moving back.

He may also tend to not stand facing you or not remain shoulders squared off with you. Turning sideways, quickly looking towards the door (revealing that he wants to get away from this situation) are all signs of reluctance or deceit.

Some people may even start to slowly move toward the exit or closer to the walls.

It's interesting to observe that all of the above reactions are very similar to how a person would react when trying to avoid *physical* harm. The primary goal is to get away from the situation/person or to run and hide so they're not 'exposed.'

Reach Out and Touch

Another thing that friends do (or at least two

people who are relaxed, confident, and forthcoming with each other) is to occasionally touch the other person's arm or shoulder, spontaneously, during conversation.

This is not something that we think about. It just happens during a positive-flowing conversation, or when we are passionate about what we are saying. (We also do this when we like the other person or are interested in them.)

Basically, the more we like the other person, and the more comfortable we are, the more touchy feely we tend to get.

On the other hand... when we have something to hide, are lying or about to lie, want to get away from the situation fast, or are holding back, we will not touch the other person very much if at all.

We will try to *increase* the distance, not get closer. And, again, we may even keep our arms very close to our body, not move it around in a relaxed manner.

(Of course, there are times when we don't

touch a person at all because we want to **hide** the fact that we *like* them. Here again, the lack of touching occurs when a person is *holding something back*.)

Shields Up

Earlier, I mentioned that a liar may often react very similar to being physically attacked, when approached with questions or accusations, i.e. he would try to get away from the situation in order to protect himself.

Additionally, he will also (without realizing) try to shield himself from you by either getting behind something (a chair, table, etc.) or by placing something between you and him (a briefcase, a child, or anything else at his disposal, really.)

This may also happen in very subtle ways, actually, which can be easy to miss if you're not paying attention.

Example: If you're both sitting down at a table, he may simply reposition a drinking glass or water pitcher by bringing it in front of him. Or even something as subtle as placing a pen or even his hands, interlaced, in front of him.

If you're standing up, moving a briefcase from his side to holding it in front of him or moving a child from his side to holding him/her directly in front of him, are giveaways of wanting to create a barrier between the two of you.

On a conscious level, we know that little things like a pen or a drinking glass will do little to protect us from an attack, physical or verbal. Yet, on an unconscious level, the mind is doing these subtle moves to protect the liar, and by doing so, it reveals his true intentions and feelings of wanting to shield himself from the other person.

Liar, Liar...Brain's on Fire

"We tell lies when we are afraid...
afraid of what we don't know, afraid
of what others will think, afraid of
what will be found out about us. But
every time we tell a lie, the thing that
we fear grows stronger."
Tad Williams

Growing up, you may have heard some old sayings like, "A thief is the first to padlock his belongings," etc.

The average person may not *always* remember to lock the front door, or activate the car alarm, or secure. We all forget sometimes.

But, interestingly enough, someone who lies, cheats or steals from others will always remember to secure his own belongings.

Why? Because, he believes that there are

thieves all around us. All the time.

Why does he think that? Because, he knows this for a fact...*he's one of them*. That's his daily reality.

The point is, a person's thought process can reveal a lot of things that he may not want known.

Also, as touched on earlier, individuals who are easily able to point out certain flaws or skews in other people (or things, situations, etc.) are often found to have those same flaws and skews within themselves.

The reason they are able to so easily spot that stuff all around them (outside of themselves) is because that same stuff is in the forefront of their own mind (inside them.) It's one of their primary focuses in life.

Obviously, this is not *always* the case. (Sometimes, a person who is quick to padlock everything may just have been a victim of theft in the past.) But, more often than not, people simply project outwardly what's going internally (inside of their own mind.)

A cheater will be quick to accuse his partner of cheating, a liar will often accuse others are lying to him and believes that the world is full of liars...and so on.

Such behaviour that reveals the person thought process should be clear red flags to you to watch the other person closely or add him to the 'suspects' list, for further study, questioning, etc.

Let's build on this and look at some examples to illustrate this phenomenon in action...

But, What Do *You* Think of Me?

Here's a subtle, but pretty significant, aspect of how a liar would speak, based on his internal focus...

When you're having a normal conversation, say with a friend, your friend may not care much about how he 'sounds' to you. He's simply immersed in the conversation. He doesn't care about whether you'd detect hidden meaning in his choice of words or sentence structure.

However, a liar will always be worried about how his conversation comes across to you. While he's supposedly talking to you, his brain is busy monitoring every word and sentence to be sure he doesn't give anything away or appear guilty to you.

Unfortunately for him, by doing so, he can easily give himself away to someone who knows what to pay attention to.

Be wary of individuals who are trying too hard to make it 'appear' as if something is a 'certain way'...whether it involves a situation, others, or about qualities within himself.

Here's an easy example...

If someone pauses a lot to carefully choose every word so that it sounds intelligent and 'smart' to you is.... 1) trying to *hide* the fact that he's insecure about his intelligence, 2) wants you to *believe* that he is intelligent, 3) generally isn't very articulate by nature and wants to mask that fact.

The above is not necessarily an example of a liar but of the person clearly trying to *hide* something...or make you believe something that isn't necessarily true (in this case, about himself.)

Here's What Happened to ME

Another way a liar is mainly focused on himself and what's going on inside his head is when his responses or statements only include what *he* was doing, seeing, feeling, etc.

The reason for this is obvious. Oftentimes, he's making his stories up as he goes along, and is so busy in trying to convince you of *his* innocence that he forgets to focus on other people.

His stories will rarely include what others were experiencing (feeling, thinking, saying.)

Example:

You: Were you at home on the night of the burglary? Your car was seen parked outside.
Him: I was at the movies...with a friend...... We went in my friend's car.

Compare the above to this one...

You: Were you at home on the night of the burglary? Your car was seen parked outside.
Him: I was at the movies, with my friend, Cindy. We took her car coz she insisted on driving because her car has a cd player and mine doesn't.

The first response may not necessarily be untrue. But, the second response just sounds more believable. The speaker pauses less, mentions his friend by name, and also reveals that his friend insisted on taking her own car, *i.e. he mentions what another person was experiencing and doing.*

Here's Why You Should *Buy*

When salespeople and marketers try to sell you something, they start by telling you about all the *benefits* of the product, they will list off every reason why the product is *great* and why you should buy it.

However, great salespeople and marketers will do it a bit differently. Aside from telling you all the great things about the product, they will *also* mention a flaw or two, i.e. something *negative* about the product.

While this may sound crazy to many, one of the reasons they mention the flaw is to make the offer appear more *believable*. If they kept telling you how great something (or someone) is, most people will start wondering if the offer sounds "too good to be true."

It works really well because 1) the marketer is being honest with you, so he can sleep well at night, and 2) you will actually appreciate the fact that he's giving you the complete story, not just the 'good parts.'

But, as mentioned earlier, *most* salespeople and marketers only talk about how great the product is...they only mention the 'positives.' They are so busy in their own head, they never realize that the offer is sounding like it's "too good to be true."

Most liars are the same way. They are trying so hard to sell you on the story that their brain is fixed on that one, single focal point...sell the story...simple, uncomplicated...*positive*. And, if they're making up the entire story, again, their brain will be too occupied with the thought of convincing you to ever do anything creative, like throwing in a few negatives in the story to make it sound more believable.

Think back to moments in your past...even during our best experiences and adventures, there tends to be at least one or two things that don't quite go right, or as we hoped they would have...be they little things or big. That's just reality.

Yet, when we have to 'make up' a story, especially on the spot, we generally tend to focus on the positive. It's easier to do that and less complex for the brain to conjure up.

Most people do the same thing when they're lying or 'making up' stories to cover something up (Unless, of course, the story has to be negatively slanted. In those cases, a liar's story may be *all* negative.)

I'm Okay, Thanks. And, How About You?

Another aspect that's common during a normal, spontaneous conversation is the back-n-forth exchange between the people talking.

When you're talking to a friend, the conversation isn't typically one-sided, i.e. one person doesn't ask all the questions while the other person simply answers (and then shuts up and waits for the next question.) That's not a conversation, that's an interrogation.

And, just as in the previous case (above,) the liar is often so busy in making up stories and lies to keep you convinced that he forgets to maintain a 'normal' conversation. In other words, he never cares enough to ask *you* any questions relating to what you just asked him.

If he does ask something that resembles his empathy toward the situation or others involved in the situation, it's possible that he's being genuine -- but not guaranteed. (He may just be a better liar than most.)

Additionally, if he doesn't ask you questions about the situation, if even it involves his own safety or negative impact, he's very likely lying or hiding something.

Example

You: Are you aware of the burglaries in your town?
Him: No, I haven't heard anything about it.
You: Three homes were broken into, within the past 5 days.
Him: Really? That's unbelievable. I'm sorry to hear that.

While the above responses may not necessarily appear suspicious, what he did *not* say (or ask) does.

You see, after hearing about a line of recent burglaries near his area, the average guy will start thinking of a dozen different questions to ask you. Questions like these...

"Which area did the break-in's happen?" (Wondering how close to his home they were.)

"What did they take?" (Wondering how serious it was and how much it could impact him.)

"Did anyone get hurt?" (Concerned about his safety and the safety of his family.)

"How did they get in?" (Wondering if his home is secure enough to withstand a burglary attempt.)

Any one of us would have similar concerns and questions.

However, a guilty person won't think to ask such questions because he's not worried about being a victim. If he is the burglar or knows something about the crimes, he's pretty sure that he won't be victimized.

Besides, his mind is too busy trying to get himself to come across as honest and innocent.

As such, it never occurs to him to *ask* certain obvious questions that the average person would be almost sure to ask. He's too busy working on *answering* your questions as convincingly as he possibly can.

Let's Move On, Already

We've already established that a liar will do his best to get the questioning over with, so that you can move on to a different subject. He may even try to change the subject himself, as quickly as possible...a clear sign that something's not right.

In addition, also pay attention to how the person *reacts* when the subject does finally change. Does he *suddenly* look relieved? Happier? Does his body (arms, hands, shoulders) open up more to match a more relaxed and relieved attitude?

Just to test this further, bring the subject back after talking a few minutes about something else. Notice how he reacts?

Does he get nervous, tense, or less cooperative once again? Does he start to answer more carefully and with more pauses again?

All of these are signs that something is up. Combined with some other signs covered in this manual, you've most likely got a liar on your hands.

But, _I_ Really Believe It!

A friend of mine, who is a family man, a Christian, and an all-around nice guy, actually told me once that he never lies, and never ever has.

Naturally, I laughed when he said that. He then went on to convince me of that fact.

After several minutes of further conversation on this fascinating subject, and some follow-up questions on my part, I realized that his _definition_ of a lie was a bit different from the average guy.

See, he felt that if what he said didn't hurt or take advantage of anyone, then it wasn't a lie at all. He actually whole-heartedly believed this to be the truth.

We can discuss further why he thought that and what may have caused him to see the world, and reality, in that way. But, that's not the objective of this manual.

My reason for bringing him up is to make you aware of certain similar cases and individuals that you may encounter in the future... a person who truly believes in the lie that he's telling. So much so that he will swear it's the absolute truth, and really mean it.

You may also encounter individuals who are pathological liars, sociopaths, etc.

Here's *Exactly* How It Happened

There are times when the person will provide an answer that sounds too good, very well rehearsed, with every detail in its place, and just...too perfect.

The person may remember details that most of us wouldn't be able to, unless we had a photographic memory. Where he was on a specific date, at a specific time, what he was wearing, what the weather was like, what and who was around him, what was playing on the radio or TV, and so on.

When asked where he was last Wednesday

at approximately 1:45 pm, he may say he was having lunch at the local deli, and then resume to pull out a receipt for said lunch, which he just happened to save.

Now...some people *may* save a receipt for a sandwich costing $5.60 from a week ago...it's possible...it can happen. But, most of us don't.

The point is, if the person's responses and actions look rehearsed and seem too perfect, it's very likely that he did in fact prepare for a situation where he'd be asked such questions. And, that is usually a huge red flag.

He Ducks, He Dodges

As touched on earlier in the manual, instead of answering your question directly, a liar may use phrases that give him the dodge and you the slip.

In addition to dodging the question with such sneaky responses, he may also be using them to stall while he thinks of a convincing lie to tell you.

Here are some commonly-used lines to watch for...

I can't believe you'd ask me that!

I'm shocked that you'd even think that!

I'm shocked that you'd ask (accuse me of) that.

Where is this coming from?

How could you think (ask me) that?

How dare you ask me something like that?

I'm not going to dignify that with a response.

I'm going to pretend I didn't hear that.

Where did you hear that?

I really don't think this is the best time (or place) to get into this.

I think we both know the answer to that.

Similarly, there are dodges done by offering *implied* answers that make you *think* that the facts are as you believe them to be.

Example...

You: You must be quite wealthy, huh?
Him: Well, everyone in my family is college-educated.

You: Do you have any problems or concerns about having a female as your superior?
Him: Oh, I've had female supervisors before. And I've also had a boss in the past that was female.

In both of the above examples, the person never really answers the question you asked him. He simply says what he is sure you'll interpret in a way that's favorable to him.

You Had Me There For A Second

Another clever way a person would dodge questions is with the use of humor. There are two primary ways he would do this...

The first way would be to act so shocked and surprised by what you asked him that he'd pause for a second and then say, "OH wait a minute...is this a joke? You're pulling a prank on me, aren't you? Ha ha very funny."

This strategy will often work because you (or whoever is asking him the question) will assume that the person couldn't possibly be guilty.

Example:

You: Do you know anything about the missing $20 from Suzie's desk?
Him: What? Are you implying that I may have stolen money from Suzie?!
You: I'm just asking if you know anything about it.
Him: Why would I know anything about.... OH wait a minute...you're messing with me, aren't you? Ha ha Very funny, dude! I almost thought for a second that you were actually accusing me of stealing! Good one!

The second way a liar could use humor to dodge the question is by replying in a humorous way from the very start...

You: Do you know anything about the missing $20 from Suzie's desk?
Him: Yes, I took it. That's what I do here...I go from desk to desk looking for cash. Then I take lunch. And then I go dumpster diving till 4:30pm. I love my job!

He may end his speech with laughter, or jokingly shake his head at you and walk away.

Both of the above methods are designed to make you feel silly (even stupid or embarrassed) for asking him the question in the first place, and possibly avoid you from doing any follow-up with him on that subject.

Sarcasm can also be used in a similar manner by the liar...

Example:

You: Do you know anything about the missing $20 from Suzie's desk?
Him: Yes, I stole it. Becoz I'm a thief. I don't make enough money so I go around stealing

from my co-workers. I steal from my children too. That's how much of a lowlife I am.

He would then give you that "I am so disgusted by you" look and walk away. He may even call you a "jerk" or something worse as he walks away.

The result would usually be the same as in the 'humor' examples above. He would leave you feeling silly, stupid or even embarrassed for ever suspecting him of stealing. And, it would also possibly deter you from asking him any other related questions.

It's Really Not That Important

This is a fairly common lying strategy that people use often without fully understanding its power and effectiveness.

Basically, the strategy is to downplay something that is actually a big deal. But, by pretending that it's nothing important, the liar hopes that you won't notice its importance and will just go along with it without questioning it further.

Example: A guy starts to tell his girl friend about something a co-worker did at work. Nothing major, just casual chatting (which is the goal.) He then casually says, "Oh yeah, Friday night, a few of us from work are going to go by Dave's place (the co-worker) after work for drinks.......If it gets a bit late, I might just crash over there for the night."

Now... if the boyfriend doesn't usually (or ever) crash at somebody else's place for the night, the girlfriend should stop to wonder about this 'casual' tidbit that he threw her way. And, if he doesn't usually hang out with his co-workers, she may have even more to be concerned about.

Aside from the above items being unusual for the boyfriend to do, he also gives himself away by **not** making a big deal out of both those situations.

See, when most of us are about to do something we don't *normally* do, we tend to talk about it...about how unusual it is, and about wondering what it might be like, what to expect, etc.

A Lie For A Lie

When I was just starting college, one of my friend's shared a powerful proverb that always stuck with me. He said, "Sometimes, a small lie can reveal some big truths."

Here's how it works...

When you start to suspect that someone may be lying to you, you don't confront him about the lie. Instead, you make up a lie yourself and see if he goes along with it. If he does, you'll know for a fact that he's a liar. (You may have seen this strategy used in movies. Script writers seem to like it.)

Example: You're at a party, and a bunch of guests (including you) end up forming a small circle and chatting with each other.

One of the guys in the group keeps trying to one-up everyone, so you decide to have some fun...

Him: Just last week, I was invited to have lunch with Bill Gates. He's got a great place.

You: No kidding. That's great. What did you think of Hammond?
Him: .... Hammond...? [he inquires...]
You: Yeah, you know, Bob Hammond? Bill's main bodyguard...that guy is like his shadow! haha
Him: Ohh.....Bob....yeah. He's...an interesting guy....
You: Yeah, he is. Did he try to squeeze your hand to mush, when he shook it? haha
Him: He *tried* to. haha

As you may have guessed by now, "Bob Hammond" does not exist. It's a fictitious character conjured up just to help your lying friend tell more lies and reveal himself.

If the guy above was being honest about his meeting with Bill Gates, he would have no reason to go along with *your* lie. He would have simply told you that he didn't meet anyone named Hammond.

The above scenario is obviously an elaborate example. (It was fitting for the above situation.) You can use much simpler lies to get the same effect.

I'm Not *That* Dumb, You Know...

Here are two ways a person could cover up a lie after he realizes that you don't believe him...

The first situation is where someone tells you a lie that isn't creative at all. Chances are, he tried to come up with a quick lie, and decided to go with the first thing that popped into his head...

Example:

You: I noticed that you weren't here last night.
Him: Yeah, sorry. Traffic was really bad, so I just gave up and went back home.
You: Traffic? Really? At 8:00pm?
Him: I'm serious, dude. If I was going to lie to you, don't think you I would have come up with a better excuse than 'traffic?'

This kind of response tends to work on most people because they do start to wonder about why the other person would use such a lame excuse, unless they were telling the truth.

The other instance is where the person goes overboard with his storytelling or excuse. And, when it is pointed out, he covers it up using a similar strategy as in the previous example...

Example:

You: I noticed that you weren't here last night.
Him: Yeah, sorry. I was on my way here when I realized I was being followed by a truck
full of gang bangers.
You: What....?
Him: It was crazy, dude. I drove around for over a half hour before I was finally able to
lose them!
You: Gang bangers? Really? And you were able to lose them...
Him: Dude, if I was going to lie to you, don't you think I would have come up with a more believable excuse than that? I'm telling you....it was crazy!

Once again, this kind of response tends to work on most people because they do start to wonder about why the other person would use such an outrageous excuse...unless it really happened.

Applying the Above Tips, Tricks and Techniques To Spot Liars

"It takes two to lie.
One to lie and one to listen. "
Homer Simpson

Think of a time when you were learning to drive a vehicle or ride a bicycle...

The first few days (or weeks) consisted of you doing each part of the process *individually*. It seemed like there were too many things to do and focus on at once, didn't it?

Yet, very soon after, you were doing everything automatically, without stopping to think about each piece of the process.

It's the same way with learning any new skill...

At first, all the tips and techniques shared in this manual may seem like a lot to remember and apply all at once. But, with practice, you can soon get to a place where it becomes a part of you; it becomes natural and automatic to notice a bunch of different movements and expressions in others, all at once.

The sooner you start practicing this out in the real world, the sooner it will become second nature to you.

What Fascinates You

It seems the most effective way to do get better at this stuff is to start with one technique or area, and as you get good at that, you can start integrating other techniques and tricks into your overall strategy.

Start with the area that interests you most. What fascinates and draws you in most about people?

If the person's facial expressions and changes intrigue you the most, start by observing that. If you're interested most in the tonal and vocal shifts of a person's speech, start there.

Now that you know what to pay attention to in each of the areas, you'll be able to see and notice clues that most people never notice, and probably never will.

And, remember...don't just focus on people's lies. It's just as important to know when a person is telling the <u>truth</u>!

That way, you'll be able to eliminate certain individuals as suspects...or you'll at least be able to notice what *changes* in them, if they *do* start lying.

Most important of all, enjoy the process!

Become interested in people. And, make it fun to learn and experiment with the above knowledge.

Printed in Great Britain
by Amazon